PERSPECTIVE WOULD HAVE US

ALSO BY ERICA CARPENTER:

*Summoned to the Fences,* Etherdome, 2002

Erica Carpenter

# Perspective Would Have Us

Burning Deck, Providence

Acknowledgments:

Grateful acknowledgement is due to the editors of *Lingo, Twenty Six,* and *No: A Journal of the Arts,* where some of these poems first appeared. Thanks also to Etherdome, publisher of *Summoned to the Fences* (2002), a chapbook in which sections of this book appeared.

Mary Barnard's *Sappho: A New Tranlsation* (University of California Press, 1958) was the source text for "Tell Everyone/ We Shall Enjoy It."

This book was made possible by a gift in memory of Toni Warren.

Burning Deck Press is the Literature Program of ANYART: CONTEMPORARY ARTS CENTER, a tax-exempt (501c3), non-profit organization.

Cover by Kristin Carlson. Bird image from "Passenger Pigeon with Match," a painting by Jeff Swanson.

for E. Carlson☙

# CONTENTS ❧

# Perspective Would Have Us ❧

## Dear A

Your contention that the character contains
blast volumes, attracting words to songs

versus my idea of personality as whirled,
like a confection, around a hollow pole.

Sensibilities may range among sweet grasses —
hardly lost, out there without us.

Poplars in the distance.

Other countries, or plain trees.

# Staged Stormfront (1)

Windows open on a code of etiquette,
deportment from a long-forgotten ravishing.
Outside, more spectral darkness
coming in a show of force.

But less exact than force:
a broad occurrence, which expects
the wrong, or most unusual,
consecutive event.

And as in waking, there is foremost
the announcement *(this,* a bedroom)

so what follows
is that prior thing, a dream.

# In that Musical Country

Relation as a violet is pressed upon a stranger's bed
repeatedly, each time resulting in an image of this city
where he finds himself in song already and in public,
being claimed like that by outside force in repetition
of his sky, his old particular positions, trees,
the reliquary lots behind each house, the rough
communicating gardens, so in time it could be
anybody passing who was summoned to those fences
and the holes through which his private world was seen.

# ROOM THIRTEEN

At the foot of the stairs one of us is talking. It is apparent to all of us he does not know what he is talking about, so when a few of us see fit to cough, we all are coughing.

Compulsively, for sake of something. Something's dry and urgent plosives. Something fiery, hung like flour.

It's sounding high and nervous like a mouse. Behind the walls, fretful but not frightening is that cleave of lath from plaster, and from nearby rooms the sound of running water. Water disports itself somewhere (behind some walls, presumably). Presumably all down birdthroats of pipes complete with rings and tags and other markings which, when drawn, communicate pure passages of love.

Someone concedes to going back against the issues
as if patient, as if clinging to a rope, a cause, a lifetime
copyright or patent, yet even now this one is picturing
a function of some spirit (he's the soul of generosity),
rising steam before his eyes.

It's like a bowl. A bowl of something.
Yes, a bowl.

Now there follows a familiar slow collapse, surface waves under surveillance of a close or passing storm. Reined in again, he is the soul of forced contrition, and before his eyes appears a certain parti-colored ball. It's a ball of a variety he's seen, perhaps he's read about, before: in books it forms round pools or near the ocean. Even he owned such a ball, once.

Neatly sectioned in its colors, like a grapefruit in its skin,
no, of course he'd never owned it. Someone else had owned
the pool, that is, the ball, or else it's everyone that owned it.
That is, it seemed so bitter in those cold extremes of grass,
and he thought he saw the ball there like a floater.
"Like a floater," as his dad was wont to say, something
sifting toward the eyes, the green, the golf course, on the sea.
A buoyant point beyond a pale and thrifty pass, it kept emerging
out where nobody could find it.

What no one owns, he says (but always quiet, sinking
quick, more like a diction rendered fat and (soft) it takes
the breath away) is mine.

He begins to think of that domain so long and yellow
after fences as a land he "mayn't be long gone to" (still
imagines that such lyrics might make sense, for once
played out across the blankets like a tiny civil war).
It reminds him of his travels in St. Louis, in St. Croix.

Of that obscure locale he can recall only one thing: a bistro painting, rather odd, which seemed to cling above a fault line on a bowstring plaster wall. A fin, an end of something, it seemed ominous and dorsal. Its subject was some animal resembling a — what? It was a walrus, with the figment of a boot around the ears, but tendered heavenward in greasy blasts of blue. He bends and sounds, suspects the bubbles in his person like a faulty hand-blown glass, attributes them to "battage,"which is local, meaning something, like the look that warns *bad soup.*

A word that sounds like what, crossed with the memory
of what he'd had for supper, every night of life in that decayed
October province would conceal its lovely name, vague as clerks
who passed him numbers in the market. Wagons passed him, he decided,
every time he closed his eyes. Otherwise it was the avenues of houses
shipping westward, below board. Hooks and grapples fastened
signage to the storefronts, and would likewise tow his body
through its complement of days.

And the ball beyond the pale, the dipper's bead and prow.

It was his luck to be that way disposed, so that the fear of integers released him nightly into ecstasies of looking, although sideways, at the blanks between the stars.

# Dear _____

We eat the biscuits even though they've left us
feeling weird and unrequited.

Friday night: now this has nothing
more to tell, my feeling full about one half

or all the time I would be vigilant and constantly
on watch.  Rather I'm speechless

where the time goes (think vibrations
at the dull end of a rope) and insist

I'm fully functional in terms and really fine.

Even tonight it must be obvious,
having started several novels,  to conclude

with our beginning other novels

## Staged Stormfront 2

A dream, so you emerge into the ordinary room
and light appears again, again it comes
in flowery deposits on the walls.

Meanwhile, another room of categories
hunkers in the paper's sought-out spot, the whorl
of ink inside the stenciled manufacturer's mistake.

The sought-out spot, the whorl.  Inside its solace
is a vertical of error, a transplant to the chamber
where detail has bottomed out.

# Dear K

I promised you a walk, and so there must have been
a park for certain moments

      nerve endings, coral,
      curving avenued interiors

but what I wanted was a house, and as I said it
ponds and grasses passing in and out of view

      fast travel, towns that beckon,
      everything but home, and yet
      expressing that idea —

To recap, it was too easy, with the black there at the edge, to
always drift toward the limits of the lawn

      beyond the green, the thought
      of light —

      whose faintest stroke
      makes up the map

## Dear Paris

This is my latest attempt to write you.

Imagine this a salutory word,
an open vista on a wilderness
or governance, the waste of time
between the index and the figure
which appoints these geese to air.

As birds in flight resemble days
or certain martyrs (thus careering
our own gaze across some order
of a table) birds themselves
resembling nothing more
than cardinal number threes.

# Birds at Heliopolis

Thought to blood must always
in possible distinction talk.

Subject to instance, substance
weight, possibly — force, always;

and where are said *breath, flight,*
always the earthbound element
claims love.

In other words (pictorial)
the difference in two hands
as pressed in prayer

and two hands flared, inverse,
the smallest digits locking wings.

Extinguished into gesture
or transfixed, some bright breast
its shelter burns

to raise its fevered image up,
that spark

# In Haven

Dawn is moving
in a low black sink. The planes continue
over straits of waves.

The roads are low, the shapes today
were reds and yellows thinking houses

> ( — dark, why pull
> perspective back there
>  like a fish?

They shut, one face
each floats.

Conceivably a place is any word or deviant,
as *dog* is bowled repeatedly across a surface water,
and *moon*, a reed, is hung above a door.

*dog:*
*moon:*
*strait:*

There are no houses in the water.

Your fish are less approachable than birds.

# Great Island

First the salvage it adheres to, then the sea
the light reflects.  The light reflects the gravity
of salvage, which is light in that condition
always shifting near the top; the salvage shifting
so the surface turns up constantly
surprised: the surface crashing
while the formal features hold.

# $\mathcal{S}$WEET $\mathcal{P}$OEMS ❦

after Fellini

$\mathcal{A}$ fish is caught.  Belly up.

Eyes the sun as if it sees itself, this matter
being hauled across a beach.

Meanwhile, what you were actually after
walks the shoal.  Perhaps you whistle.

A buoy rides the shoulder of a wave
or breaks behind it.

The signal is as always,
getting drowned out by the wind.

When death arrives it shapes the body
to the uses of an angel.

this was noted in the specter
of the fish, which being human
we'd mistaken for a sign.

Call it an angel, no one would
take a thing for granted.

       it's the nearness of divinity
       that makes us act so brutal —
       seeing we can only suffer
       in comparison.

Some men can't abide the sound of wind
played back.

> he might have swallowed fishes whole,
> a crime reflecting his desire for absolutes,
> who cannot see beyond the carcass
> or the leering of the crowd.

No one felt worse about those little deaths,
but this cannot excuse becoming a PR man in our eyes.

      that monster dying on the beach
      is not the same as an American
      film actress, and in different ways
      exceeds the size of life.

And who would not descend
to prostitutes, given opportunity?


      like suicide, this might be just another way
      of pulling bodies out of water
      in order to experience the earth, in all its force.

## Parallax

Something lapses into view, flashing
its longest profile, full to the depth
of a cove at the back of the eye, equally far
as it throws itself out.  Like this, a stalled wave
or photograph held, its image obstructing
the lungs of the mind, something caught
in the drafts of its own receding, permanent
uptake of light into air

# Dear X

Returned to bed for light, the silver necklace
and the fan, black gloss of leaves pretend
a green that feels like summer

Trees less monstrous than recalled; instead
this sense of having once been more among them,
as a cast bird on a table may seem
closer when a person is alone

No one's discovered how we must expand
into the shrinking of the world
except the body, in its certainty and girth

# Two Minutes Later

Darkness kept, even with the streetlights,
holding constantly erect, so that the boulevards could perish
into frames of passing cars.

# Fragment: It's No Use

It's no use Mother I
Mother can't finish my
it's no [soft] I

weaving. You may can't
my [killed] blame
Aphrodite, weaving

Soft as she is (has almost
[soft] me with [killed]
for that —

she has almost [killed]
me with [soft])
for that boy

# Ask the Phoenix

how long, to travel
into one death
and find another,
repeatedly

# Phoenix Replies

till joys cease
and woe
puts out fires
and frost
comforts

# TELL EVERYONE /
# WE SHALL ENJOY IT ❧

After Sappho

Rain penetrates
the nightingale's
last night —

today I've watched
persuasion's varied
signatures in time

Rich as you are,
you are still headed
for disaster.

At the height of honor,
something else will either
have to finish all your projects

or else desire you,
and so completely

you will want
no share in roses

―――――――――――――――

I took my lyre and said
in afternoon

I hear them chanting

At my age — well,
things were different.

This way, that way
my lovely friends and I.

Of course I love you, but I
hear that girl Andromeda
is well

—————————————————

Standing by my bed,
I asked myself and said
I will confess: it's noontime

Really darling, as you love me
and are rich, please do not ask me
what to wear.

I have no thought remaining
for the laborers in Sardis
or the children in the mills.

These days my seriousness
goes toward wherever
you are standing

_____

It's no use: people gossip.

*Peace reigned in heaven*

And my mother always said
a purple ribbon would bring dignity
to tawdry situations

looped around my head

I am less ready to be married here
than borne away by air

———————————————

*on the morning I saw —*

But then you are the herdsman
of the evening.

We should sleep.

But we've grown dark

and what was fine to us
now fails with us

as flowers fail, compared
to torchlight

———————————

Clumsy girl, tomorrow
you had better hide that urn
inside a cupboard.

Or we'll break it.

Do you remember?

I told you once
what you remind me of
when sleepy

——————————————————

Cyprian, my dreams are
as those grasses

Gods have blessed you,
nearly as often
as I've asked you

do the same for me

_____

And their movements
crush a circlet
for my head

## A Minute Waltz

compared to a dance, it's pronounced pretty.

it's nine o'clock.

it's midnight under the potsherds
of the previous day.

to go all day without touching, and the corse
laid on the threshold.

then meeting again, in passages.

# Base

night ends inconclusively,
planes trawling cross
the bar, the basin of the heavens
duplicates the harbor base,
a low black sink and nothing;
nothing rising but the ribs,
in waves drawn out
like pleating, satin black
departing skiffs disturb

# Parallax ii

Equally far as it throws itself out, the eye
tracking patterns in intimate forms,
long as the lines will hold. Where light
in the last sense may be the wrong term:
light, fair and idle while other subjects
will tend to decline, and what charge inhabits
the trees in the cove at the back of the mind,
that circle attracting the body down (down
in the sense that perspective would have us
eternally growing smaller)

# Suspense,

or this attempt to attenuate longing
into something more practical, a fan of nerves
or coral passed through daylit water —

I keep thinking of the Jamestown bridge
but there's no relation to you and me.

Still waiting for someone to explain that dream
of the boat that capsized underneath, everyone trying
to climb on top where the keel bellied up like a fish.

A few yards off you're sinking in slowly, an elegant film fade
to waters below. You tell us at least you might find the dog.

Or the one where the road had fallen away.
We crawled along cables to get there.

# Dear Y

About the body, I've acquired one.
I hold a late confusion which was obdurate
responsible. I admit to feeling more a member now,
much more at home in public, but still I can attest
to certain loss. The old obsessions, less condensed,
are drifting outward from the primal constellation.
Where they touch on the apparent there's no bothering
with thrills, crows, knells. Even the streets are low
and conscious of the blackness that's dispersed
amidst the grass on axis days, the early cold
of early cold.

# Communiqué

Sickness and the menu sifted down again
to questions which pertained to how she lived.
On the road and in the middle of America, she said
a rough interior plots notions further out.
She mentioned shapes in giant fields,
unsummarizable you'd swear except
from windows in a plane, and then
she cinched them into names
that you could crawl through.

(about your sensitive equipment,
she delivered no report)

# SIX VIEWS FROM CAPRI

After Godard

*O* what world is this.

Paul is working on his screenplay,
and so forsakes Camille.

Love dies underwater.

Eternally, Camille
will be remembered by Paul
and all the others as a body

borne on undulating shag,
immoderately white.

All of this is held somewhere
within the basin of experience.

What gets tricky is not so much
the past as this contagious sense
of history;

call it narrative potential,
or an eye for combinations.

For instance: I do not know Paul.

How can I know that Paul's a hack?

It's enough just to be open to the cues.

Now, the event lies always curled
within the lip of history, and is likewise
its own lip.

In the dark, in rows, in ordinary velvet,
you and I believe that we are poised
between the teeth, and love dies in glory
on the freeway.

Still, do I know Paul?

Paul falls within the genre
of the thriller: though not overly complex,
can be exciting and a beast.

And Camille?
Camille is an apartment.

Worse, she's trapped
inside an art film in the '60s.

All that I require of this life
may be an airport-style,
avant-garde, red acrylic couch.

A modular beauty, like Camille
had in the film —

forgetting here we have
no confidence in sectionals.

# Catalog

This image has no depth, compared
to older processes (silvery, abandoned
at an elbow in the bank). Slivers in the light, also the details
are incongruous: a hand emerging flaglike
from a field like shattered glass. So you're inclined
to ponder where, when, and under what conditions
such a thing is likely, also a flightless creature
that was stationed on your roof. It walked around at night,
its footsteps telling where you were inside a house
and with regard to what it seemed could not be shown.
This image, depthless, shivers near the banks of recognition.
Beyond a point it breaks up harmlessly against the shoreline rocks.
A boy and girl could stand for hours in such
a natural arrangement: afternoon
a finished image lodged inside one half
of each their minds. It has no depth,
you can see it's neither water nor a river,
how they go on diving in.

# Parallax iii

the charge that inhabits
the trees in the shade at the back
of a field, at the end of a view where the eye
travels down or is pulled, where the eye
becomes target of objects (this cove in its depth
of reflected trees) existing in seeming to hold
to themselves, themselves as a body explained.

This book was designed and computer type-set by Rosmarie Waldrop in 10 pt. Palatino with Phyllis initials. Printed on 55 lb. Writers' Natural (an acid-free paper), smyth-sewn and glued into paper covers by McNaughton & Gunn in Saline, Michigan. The cover by Kristin Carlson uses an image from Jeff Swanson's painting, "Passenger Pigeon with Match." There are 1000 copies, of which 50 are numbered & signed.